PARES SCALES

For Individual Study
and Like-Instrument Class Instruction

by GABRIEL PARÈS

Revised and Edited by Harvey S. Whistler

Published for:

Flute or Piccolo . . . . Parès-Whistler

Clarinet . . . . Parès-Whistler

Oboe . . . . Parès-Whistler

● Bassoon . . . . Parès-Whistler

Saxophone . . . . Parès-Whistler

Cornet, Trumpet or Baritone 𝄞 . . . . Parès-Whistler

French Horn, E♭ Alto or Mellophone . . . . Parès-Whistler

Trombone or Baritone 𝄢 . . . . Parès-Whistler

E♭ Bass . . . . Parès-Whistler

BB♭ Bass . . . . Parès-Whistler

Marimba, Xylophone or Vibes . . . . Parès-Whistler-Jolliff

For Individual Study and Like-Instrument Class Instruction
(Not Playable by Bands or by Mixed-Instruments)

RUBANK®

HAL•LEONARD®
CORPORATION

7777 W. BLUEMOUND RD. P.O. BOX 13819 MILWAUKEE, WI 53213

Key of C Major

Long Tones to Strengthen Lips

Also practice holding each tone for EIGHT counts.
When playing long tones, practice (1) ⟨ and (2) ⟨⟩.

3

Embouchure Studies

Slur as many tones as possible. Also practice tonguing each tone.

Slur as many tones as possible. Also practice tonguing each tone.

Key of F Major

Long Tones to Strengthen Lips

Scale of F

Also practice holding each tone for EIGHT counts.
When playing long tones, practice (1) ⟨ and (2) ⟨ ⟩ .

Embouchure Studies

Slur as many tones as possible. Also practice tonguing each tone.

Slur as many tones as possible. Also practice tonguing each tone.

Key of G Major

Long Tones to Strengthen Lips

Scale of G

Also practice holding each tone for EIGHT counts.
When playing long tones, practice (1) ⟨ and (2) ⟨ ⟩.

Embouchure Studies

Slur as many tones as possible. Also practice tonguing each tone.

Slur as many tones as possible. Also practice tonguing each tone.

Key of B♭ Major
Long Tones to Strengthen Lips

Scale of B♭

Also practice holding each tone for EIGHT counts.

When playing long tones, practice (1) ⎯◁ and (2) ◁▷

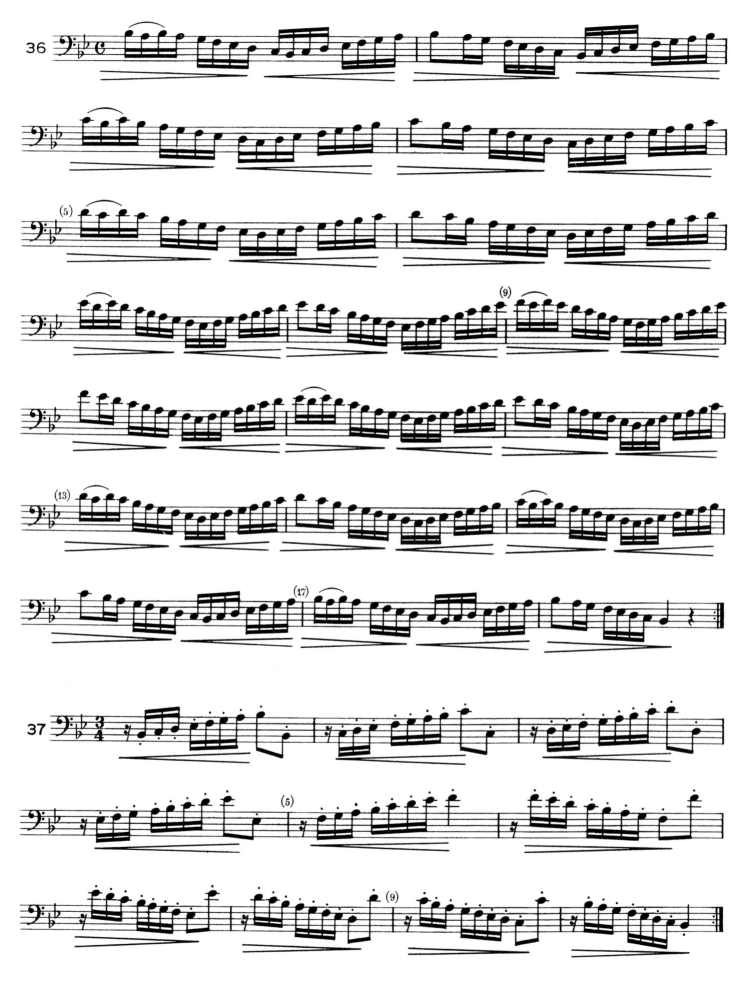

Embouchure Studies

Slur as many tones as possible. Also practice tonguing each tone.

Slur as many tones as possible. Also practice tonguing each tone.

Key of D Major

Long Tones to Strengthen Lips

Scale of D

42

Also practice holding each tone for EIGHT counts.
When playing long tones, practice (1) ⟨ and (2) ⟨ ⟩ .

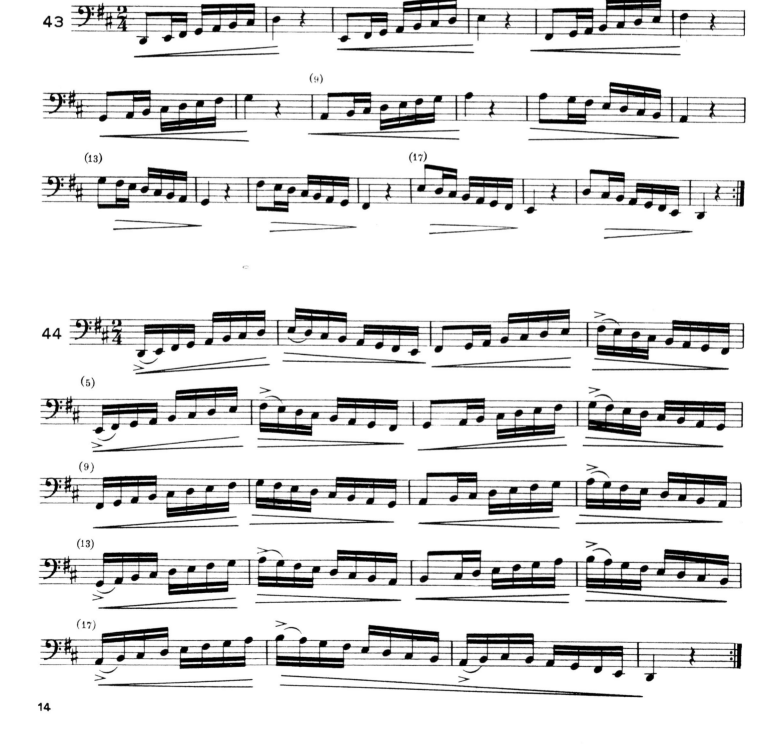

Embouchure Studies

Slur as many tones as possible. Also practice tonguing each tone.

Slur as many tones as possible. Also practice tonguing each tone.

Key of E♭ Major

Long Tones to Strengthen Lips

Also practice holding each tone for EIGHT counts.
When playing long tones, practice (1) ⦟ and (2) ⦟⦠.

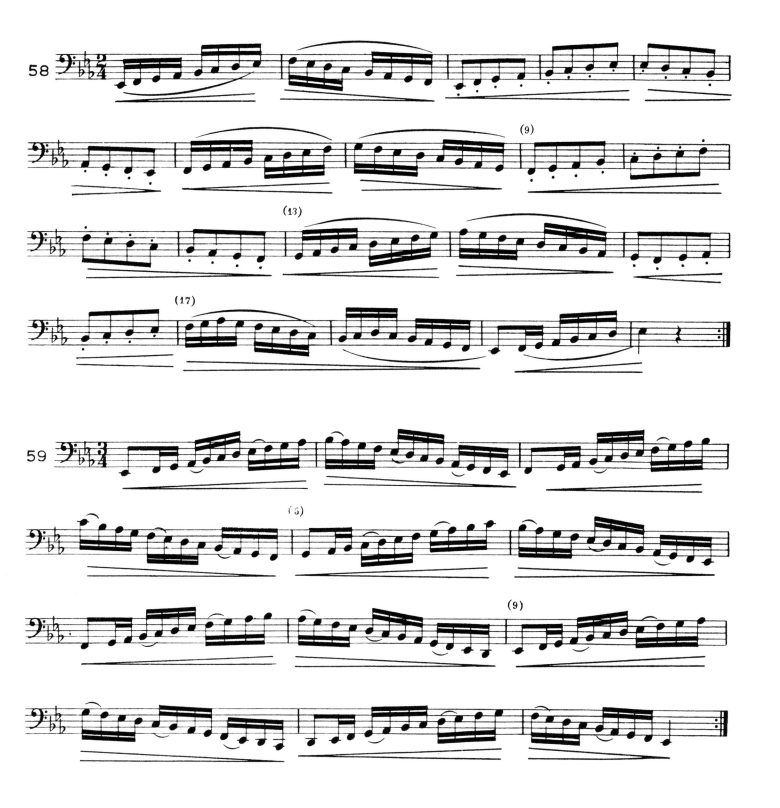

Embouchure Studies

Slur as many tones as possible. Also practice tonguing each tone.

Slur as many tones as possible. Also practice tonguing each tone.

Key of A Major
Long Tones to Strengthen Lips

Also practice holding each tone for EIGHT counts.

When playing long tones, practice (1) ⟨ and (2) ⟨⟩.

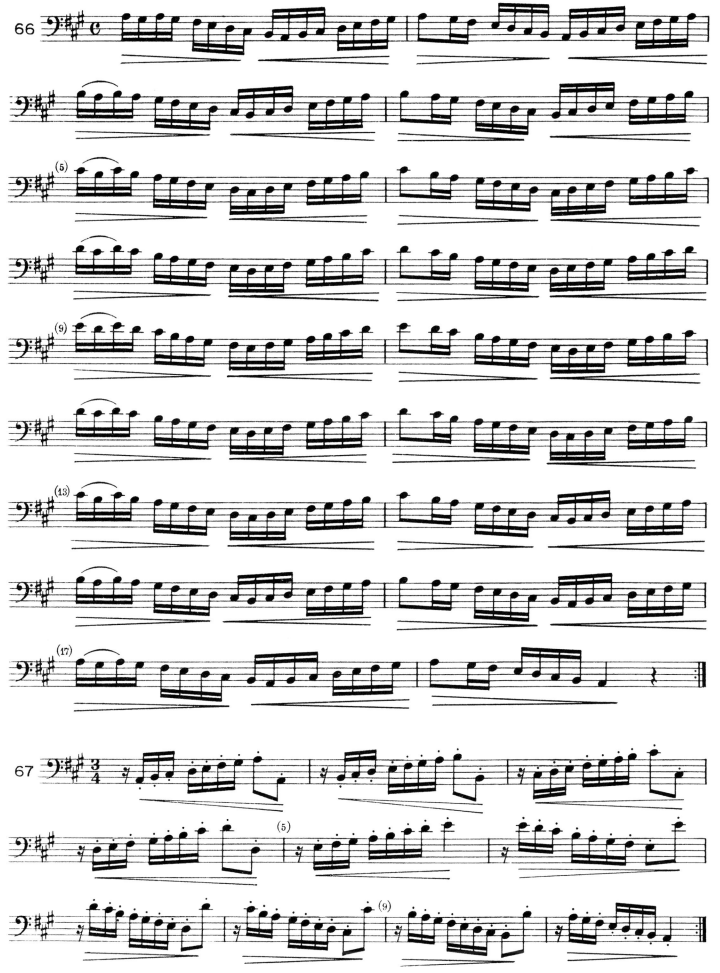

Embouchure Studies

Slur as many tones as possible. Also practice tonguing each tone.

Slur as many tones as possible. Also practice tonguing each tone.

Key of A♭ Major

Long Tones to Strengthen Lips

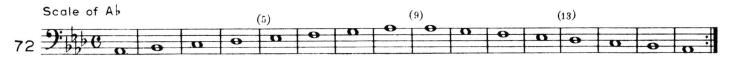

72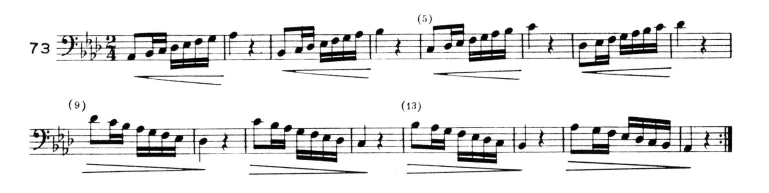

Also practice holding each tone for EIGHT counts.
When playing long tones, practice (1) ⟨ and (2) ⟨⟩

73

74

75

Embouchure Studies

Slur as many tones as possible. Also practice tonguing each tone.

Slur as many tones as possible. Also practice tonguing each tone.

Key of D♭ Major

Long Tones to Strengthen Lips

83

Also practice holding each tone for EIGHT counts
When playing long tones, practice (1) $\longleftarrow$ and (2) $\longleftarrow$.

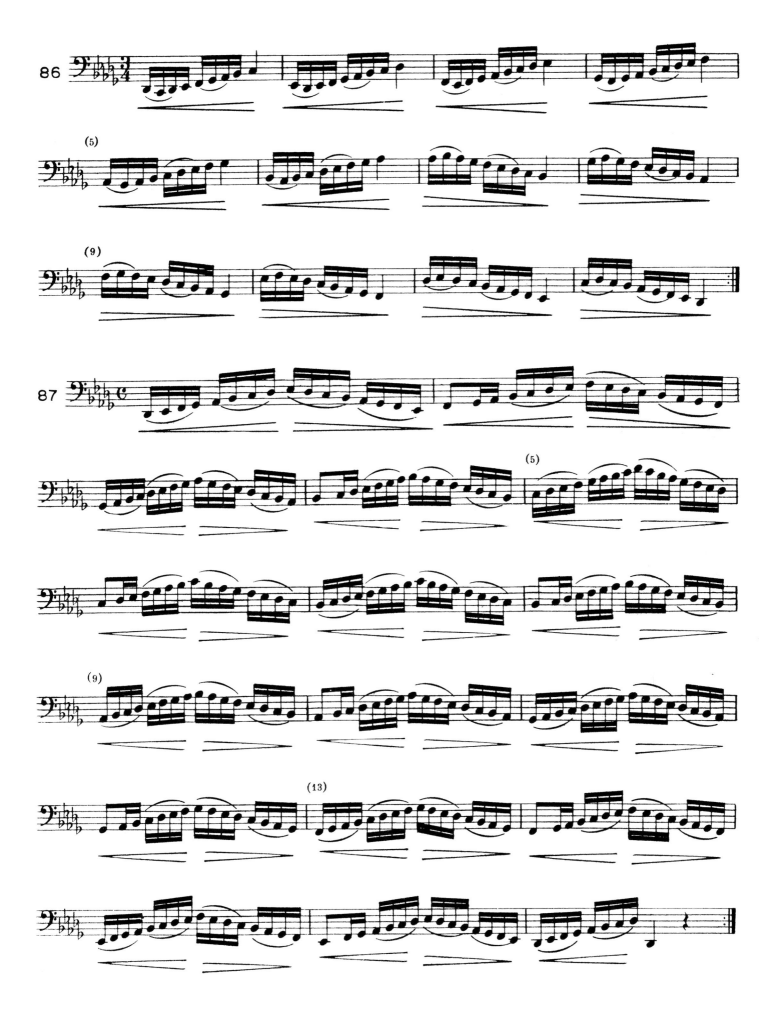

Embouchure Studies

Slur as many tones as possible. Also practice tonguing each tone.

Slur as many tones as possible. Also practice tonguing each tone.

Key of A Minor
(Relative to the Key of C Major)

Long Tones to Strengthen Lips

Also practice holding each tone for EIGHT counts.

When playing long tones, practice (1) and (2).

Embouchure Studies

Slur as many tones as possible. Also practice tonguing each tone.

Slur as many tones as possible. Also practice tonguing each tone.

Key of D Minor

(Relative to the Key of F Major)

Long Tones to Strengthen Lips

Scale of D Harmonic Minor

Scale of D Melodic Minor

Also practice holding each tone for EIGHT counts.
When playing long tones, practice (1) $\longleftarrow$ and (2) $\longleftrightarrow$.

Embouchure Studies

Slur as many tones as possible. Also practice tonguing each tone.

Slur as many tones as possible. Also practice tonguing each tone.

Key of E Minor
(Relative to the Key of G Major)

Long Tones to Strengthen Lips

Scale of E Harmonic Minor

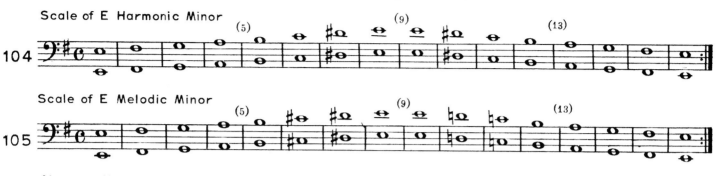

104

Scale of E Melodic Minor

105

Also practice holding each tone for EIGHT counts.
When playing long tones, practice (1) ⟨ and (2) ⟨⟩ .

106

107

Embouchure Studies

Slur as many tones as possible. Also practice tonguing each tone.

108

Slur as many tones as possible. Also practice tonguing each tone.

109

Key of G Minor

(Relative to the Key of B Major)

Long Tones to Strengthen Lips

Scale of G Harmonic Minor

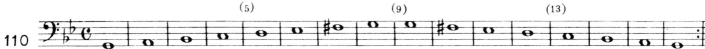

Scale of G Melodic Minor

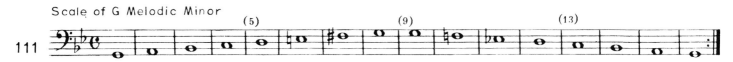

Also practice holding each tone for EIGHT counts.
When playing long tones, practice (1) and (2)

Embouchure Studies

Slur as many tones as possible. Also practice tonguing each tone.

Slur as many tones as possible. Also practice tonguing each tone.

Key of B Minor

(Relative to the Key of D Major)

Long Tones to Strengthen Lips

Scale of B Harmonic Minor

116

Scale of B Melodic Minor

117

Also practice holding each tone for EIGHT counts.

When playing long tones, practice (1) ⟨⟩ and (2) ⟨⟩

118

119

Embouchure Studies

Slur as many tones as possible. Also practice tonguing each tone.

120

Slur as many tones as possible. Also practice tonguing each tone.

121

Key of C Minor

(Relative to the Key of E♭ Major)

Long Tones to Strengthen Lips

Scale of C Harmonic Minor

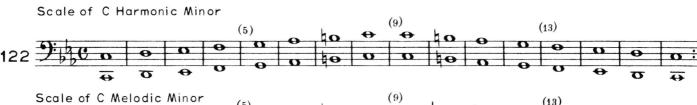

Scale of C Melodic Minor

Also practice holding each tone for EIGHT counts.
When playing long tones, practice (1) ⋖ and (2) ⋖ ⋗

Embouchure Studies

Slur as many tones as possible. Also practice tonguing each tone.

Slur as many tones as possible. Also practice tonguing each tone.

Key of F# Minor
(Relative to the Key of A Major)

Long Tones to Strengthen Lips

Scale of F# Harmonic Minor

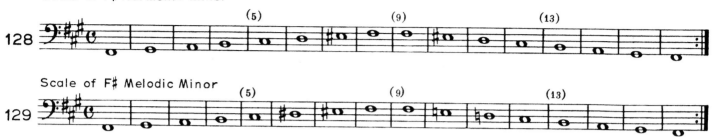

Also practice holding each tone for EIGHT counts
When playing long tones, practice (1) ⟨ and (2) ⟨

Embouchure Studies

Slur as many tones as possible. Also practice tonguing each tone.

Slur as many tones as possible. Also practice tonguing each tone.

Key of F Minor
(Relative to the Key of A♭ Major)
Long Tones to Strengthen Lips

Scale of F Harmonic Minor

134

Scale of F Melodic Minor

135

Also practice holding each tone for EIGHT counts.

When playing long tones, practice (1) and (2)

136

137

Embouchure Studies

Slur as many tones as possible. Also practice tonguing each tone.

138

Slur as many tones as possible. Also practice tonguing each tone.

139

Key of B♭ Minor
(Relative to the Key of D♭ Minor)
Long Tones to Strengthen Lips

Scale of B♭ Harmonic Minor

Scale of B♭ Melodic Minor

Also practice holding each tone for EIGHT counts.

When playing long tones, practice (1) ⬦ and (2) ⬦

Embouchure Studies

Slur as many tones as possible. Also practice tonguing each tone.

Slur as many tones as possible. Also practice tonguing each tone.

Major Scales

Harmonic Minor Scales

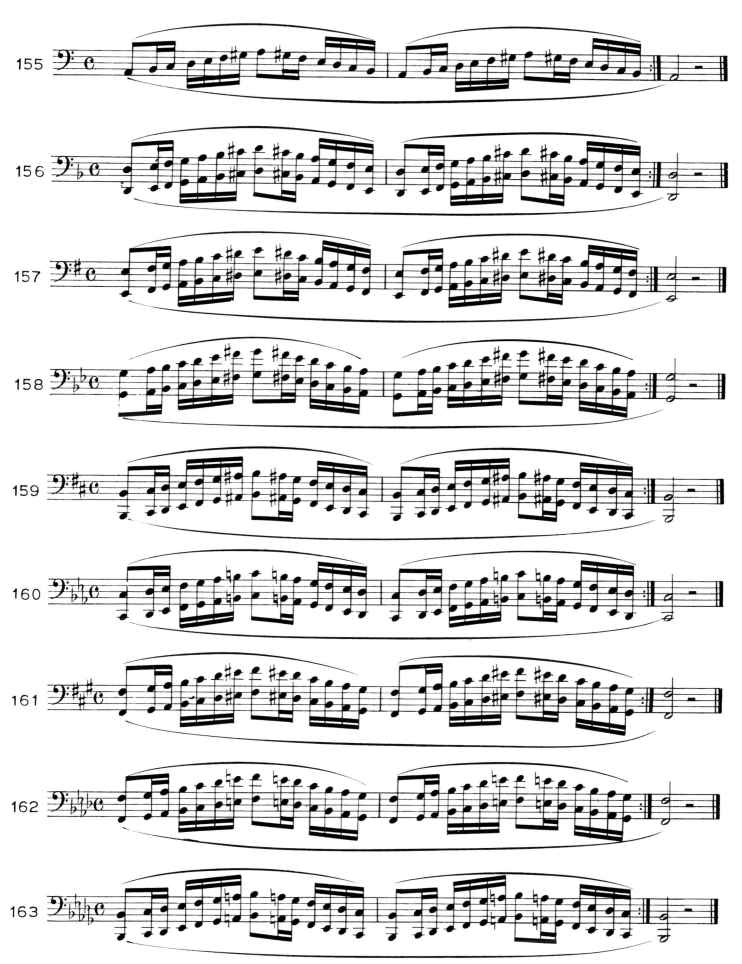

Melodic Minor Scales

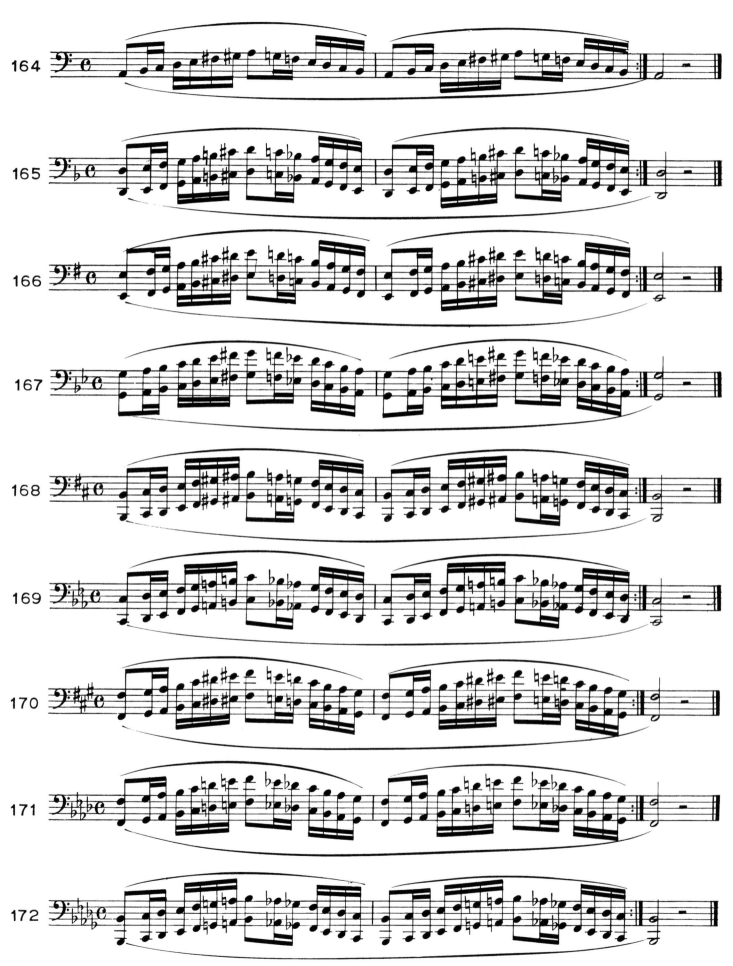

Arpeggios

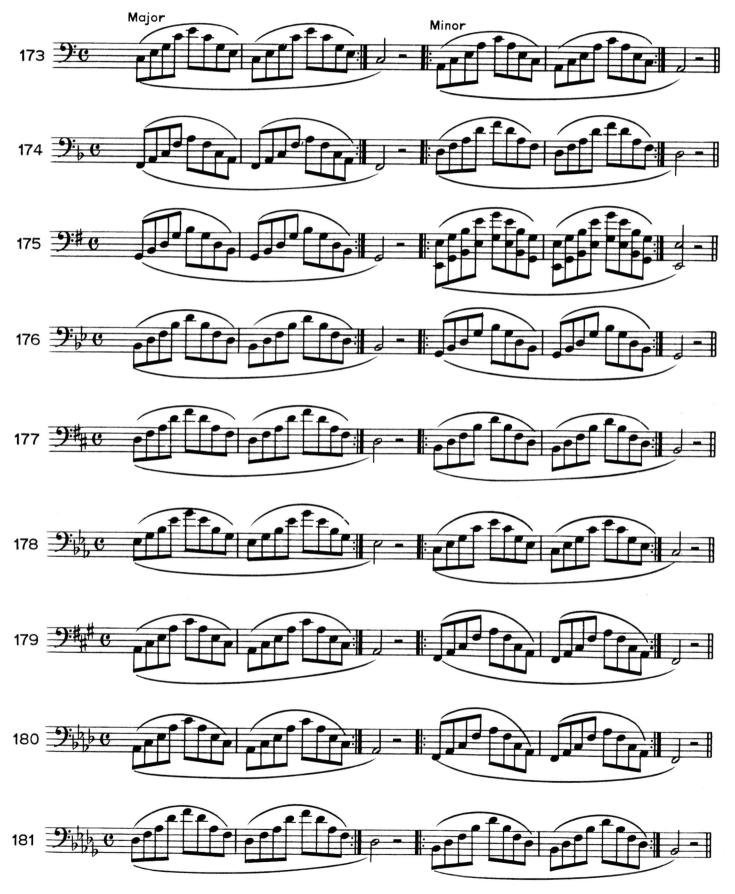

Half-Hole Finger Technic

Half-Hole Foundation Studies

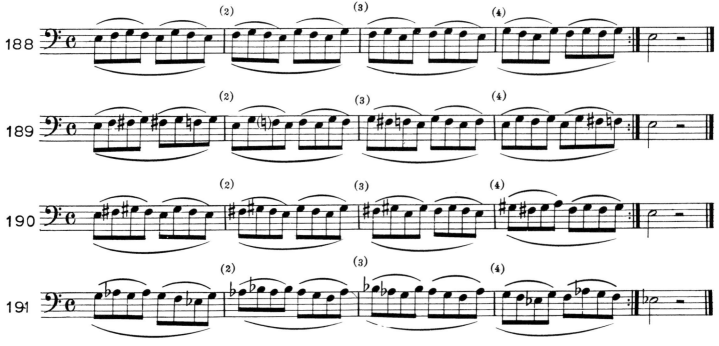

Chromatic Exercises

Chromatic Scales in Triplets

Basic Exercises to Strengthen Low Tones

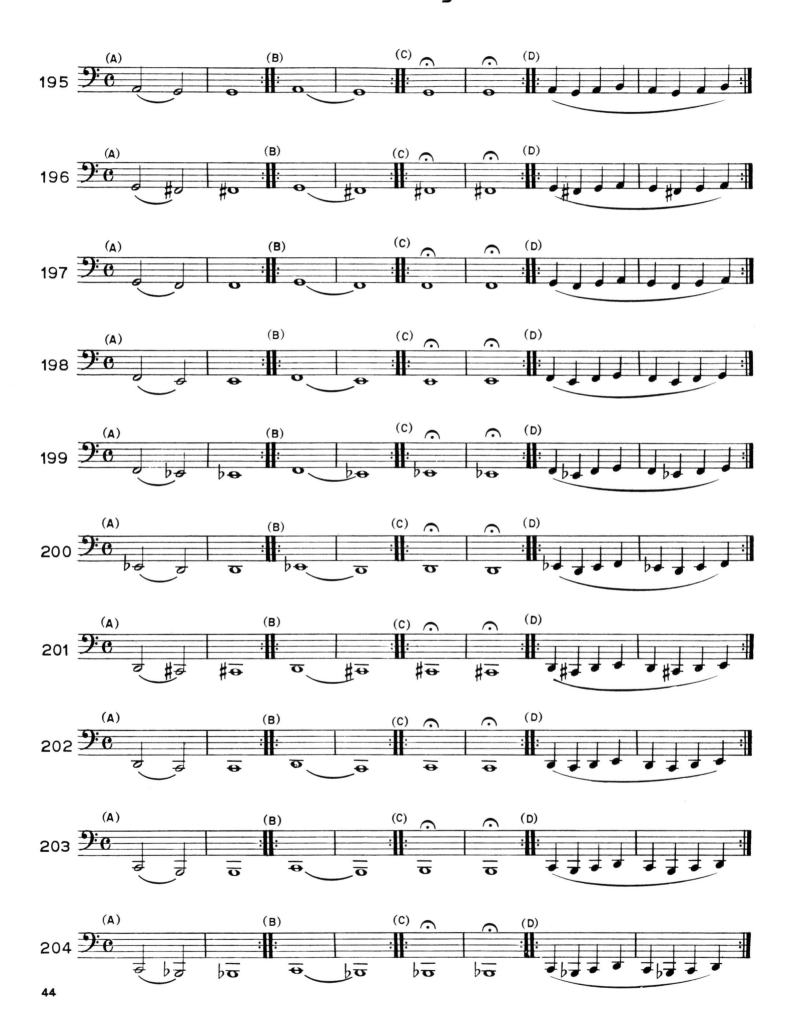

Basic Exercises to Strengthen High Tones

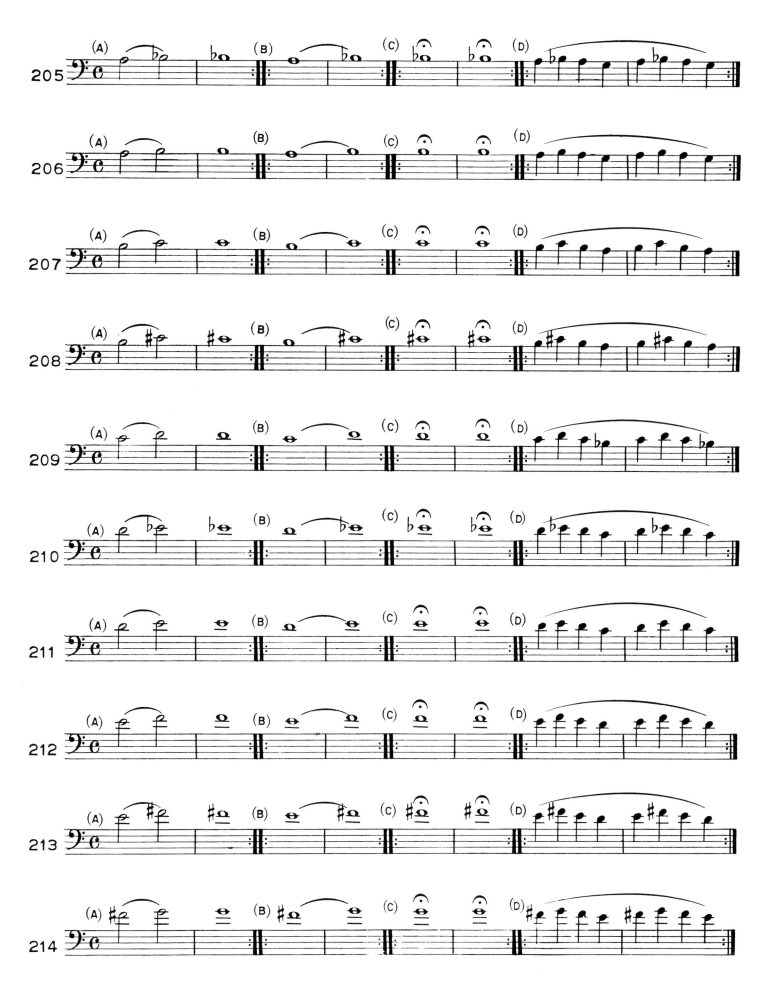

Foundation Study

Velocity Study

Artist Etude

Technic Builder No.1

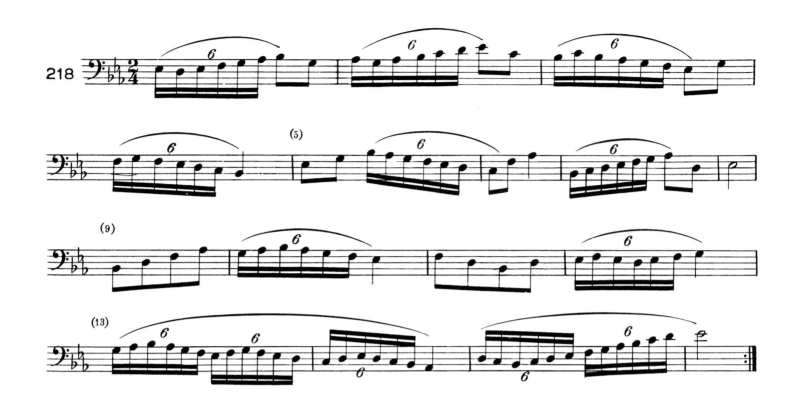

Technic Builder No.2

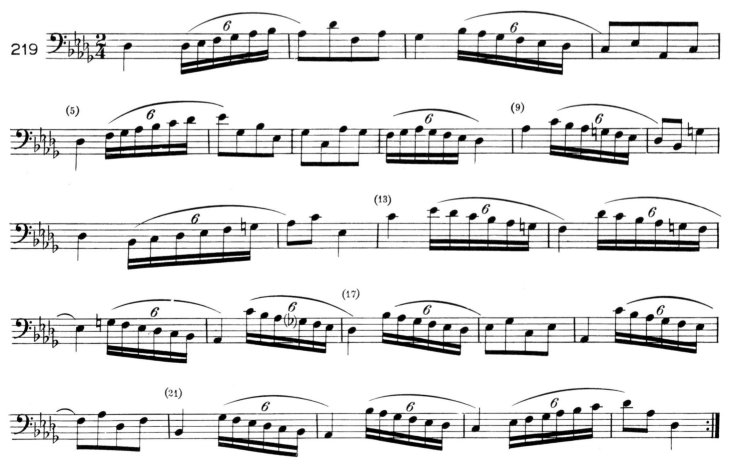